ELON MUSK
A BIOGRAPHY OF AN ENTREPRENEUR AND INNOVATOR

ROSS DANVERS

CONTENTS

INTRODUCTION

In the pantheon of contemporary entrepreneurs and visionaries, few figures are as compelling and polarizing as Elon Musk. "Elon Musk: A Biography of an Entrepreneur and Innovator" delves into the life of a man whose name is synonymous with the cutting edge of technological advancement and entrepreneurial daring. From his early life in South Africa to his emergence as a defining figure in the digital age, Musk's journey is a testament to the power of relentless ambition and visionary foresight.

This concise biography aims to capture the essence of Musk's multifaceted life: his formative years that shaped his relentless drive, his initial forays into the world of entrepreneurship, and the sprawling empire of innovation he has since built. Musk's ventures—Tesla Motors, SpaceX, Neuralink, SolarCity—each represent monumental shifts in their respective fields, from automotive and space travel to energy and beyond. Yet, beyond the entrepreneur and innovator is a complex individual, whose personal life and philosophy offer insight into the man behind the headlines.

Through chapters dedicated to each significant period and aspect of Musk's life, this biography paints a portrait of a man who refuses to accept the status quo. From his childhood dreams and early ventures to his ambitions in reshaping transportation, both on Earth and in space, and his controversial acquisition of Twitter, Musk's story is one of perpetual motion towards a future only he seems to fully envision.

"Elon Musk: A Biography of an Entrepreneur and Innovator" also explores Musk's unique approach to leadership and his personal philosophy, shedding light on how these elements have contributed to his unparalleled success in business. It delves into his personal life, from his relationships to his family, providing a more rounded understanding of the individual beyond his public persona.

As we look towards what the future holds for Elon Musk, it's clear that his impact on the world is far from over. His ventures continue to push the boundaries of what's possible, challenging us to reimagine our limitations and the potential for human achievement. This biography is not just the story of a remarkable entrepreneur and innovator; it's an exploration of what drives one man to change the world and how, in doing so, he has inspired countless others to believe in the seemingly impossible.

CHAPTER 1: THE FORMATIVE YEARS

In the heart of Pretoria, South Africa, on June 28, 1971, Elon Reeve Musk was born into a world brimming with the complex heritage and tumultuous history of his native country. The son of Maye Musk, a model and dietitian from Regina, Saskatchewan, Canada, and Errol Musk, a South African electromechanical engineer, pilot, and sailor, Elon's lineage was as diverse as his future ambitions. This mix of backgrounds, cultures, and disciplines in his family perhaps foreshadowed the eclectic range of interests and ventures that would define his career.

Elon's early life was characterized by a confluence of contrasting experiences, from the serene landscapes of South Africa to the complexities of its socio-political environment. Growing up in a household that valued intellectual pursuits and creativity, Musk showed an early proclivity for the sciences and a deep curiosity about the universe. However, his childhood was not without its challenges. His parents divorced when he was ten, an event that marked a turning point in his young life, leading him to spend more time immersed in books and computers.

From a young age, Musk was an avid reader, delving into a wide range of subjects from science fiction to philosophy. His voracious reading habit was not just an escape but a way to explore and understand the world beyond the immediate confines of his surroundings.

Early Entrepreneurship

Elon Musk's early venture into the world of technology and entrepreneurship began with his creation and sale of Blastar, a simple space-themed video game, at the tender age of 12. This early achievement not only showcased his precocious talent in programming but also hinted at the relentless drive and innovative spirit that would define his later endeavors.

The story of Blastar begins in the early 1980s, in the midst of a burgeoning computer revolution. Personal computers were becoming increasingly accessible to the general public, and with this new technology came a growing interest in computer programming. It was during this era of technological optimism that a young Elon Musk, already an avid reader and self-taught learner, turned his attention to computers.

Musk's interest in programming was sparked by a desire to understand how computers worked and what could be done with them. With no formal training in computer science, he taught himself programming using a manual on the BASIC programming language. This self-directed learning was characteristic of Musk's approach to education; he sought out knowledge not just for academic achievement but out of a genuine curiosity about the world.

Diving into the world of coding, Musk set out to create his own video game. The game, named Blastar, was a simple but functional space shooter game inspired by the science fiction books and movies he loved. Players controlled a spaceship, aiming to destroy enemy ships and avoid space mines. Despite its simplicity, Blastar was a significant accomplishment for a 12-year-old, demonstrating not only Musk's grasp of programming but also his creativity and ability to complete a project from concept to execution.

Seeking to share his creation with the world, Musk took the step of selling Blastar. He compiled the source code and instructions, and managed to sell the game to a magazine called PC and Office Technology for approximately $500. The magazine published the code, allowing other enthusiasts to type it into their own computers to play the game.

This early success was more than just a childhood achievement; it was a glimpse into Musk's future. The sale of Blastar foreshadowed Musk's entrepreneurial spirit, showcasing his willingness to innovate and his desire to make his ideas a reality.

Education

Musk was enrolled in Waterkloof House Preparatory School and later attended Pretoria Boys High School, one of the area's most prestigious secondary schools. Even as a student, Elon was markedly different from his peers. His insatiable appetite for knowledge set him apart early on. He was exceptionally curious, with a keen interest in a wide range of subjects, especially physics, computer science, and anything related to space and technology.

Despite his intellectual pursuits, school was not always a positive experience for Musk. Reports from his time in school describe him as a reserved and introspective student, traits that made him a target for bullies. Musk's brother, Kimbal, has recounted instances of bullying that Elon faced, including a particularly severe incident that resulted in Elon being hospitalized after being pushed down a staircase. These experiences of bullying were distressing, yet they arguably contributed to Musk's resilience and determination.

In the realm of academics, Musk was a high achiever. His propensity for self-learning allowed him to excel in subjects that interested him, particularly science and computer programming. However, Musk's academic journey was not without its struggles. His deep interest in certain areas sometimes came at the expense of others, leading to a somewhat uneven academic record. Yet, even in this context, Musk's ability to focus intensely on his passions was evident, a trait that would serve him well in his future entrepreneurial endeavors.

Moving Abroad

Elon Musk's decision to move abroad after high school was a pivotal moment in his life, one driven by a combination of personal ambition, a quest for greater opportunities, and a desire to escape the confines of his then-present circumstances in South Africa. This decision marked the beginning of Musk's journey from a curious, ambitious student to a global entrepreneur and visionary.

Several factors contributed to Musk's decision to leave South Africa. Firstly, there was his inherent desire to explore opportunities beyond what he perceived as the limitations of his home country. Musk was deeply aware of the technological innovations and entrepreneurial spirit flourishing in other parts of the world, particularly in the United States, which he saw as the forefront of possibilities in technology and space exploration.

Moreover, South Africa's political climate at the time, including the system of apartheid, played a significant role in his decision. Musk was opposed to the apartheid regime, and the prospect of mandatory service in the South African military, which upheld apartheid policies, was unpalatable to him. He sought a future where he could work on projects that aligned with his values and ambitions, without being complicit in a system he did not agree with.

Musk's first step in his journey abroad was to move to Canada. In 1989, at the age of 17, he made the decision to leave South Africa. This move was strategic, leveraging his mother's Canadian citizenship to gain entry into a country that offered more opportunities and served as a stepping-stone to eventually moving to the United States.

Upon arriving in Canada, Musk faced numerous challenges. He initially stayed with a relative in Saskatchewan, but the transition was far from smooth. Musk undertook a series of odd jobs, including tending vegetables at a cousin's farm and cleaning boilers at a lumber mill, to support himself. These early experiences in Canada were a testament to his resilience and determination, traits that would serve him well in his future entrepreneurial endeavors.

University

Musk began his higher education at Queen's University in Kingston, Ontario, Canada, in 1989. Queen's University is one of Canada's leading institutions, and Musk's time there, though brief, was an important step in his academic and professional development.

At Queen's, Musk was known to be focused and driven, already exhibiting a keen interest in business and technology. However, his stay at Queen's University was relatively short-lived, as he transferred to the University of Pennsylvania after two years. This decision was motivated by his desire to delve deeper into his areas of interest and to position himself closer to the epicenter of technological innovation in the United States.

In 1992, Musk transferred to the University of Pennsylvania (Penn), an Ivy League university known for its strong programs in both sciences and business. At Penn, he pursued a dual bachelor's degree program, earning a Bachelor of Science in Physics from the College of Arts and Sciences and a Bachelor of Science in Economics from the Wharton School. This dual focus mirrored Musk's interests in both the theoretical underpinnings of the universe, as well as the practical aspects of business and entrepreneurship.

Musk's choice of physics and economics as his areas of study is reflective of his broad-ranging intellectual curiosity and his ambition to address some of the most pressing challenges facing humanity. Physics provided him with a deep understanding of the natural world, which would later inform his ventures in space exploration through SpaceX. Economics, on the other hand, equipped him with insights into the functioning of markets and businesses, which would be crucial in his leadership of companies like Tesla, SolarCity, and PayPal.

Elon Musk's university years were marked not just by academic pursuits but also by his early entrepreneurial activities. He and a fellow student rented a large house off-campus, turning it into an unofficial nightclub. This venture was one of Musk's first forays into entrepreneurship, showcasing his knack for identifying opportunities and his willingness to take risks. The endeavor was reportedly quite successful, helping Musk make ends meet during his time at Penn.

Despite his business activities, Musk remained deeply engaged in his studies. His time at Penn was characterized by a rigorous academic workload, which he managed alongside his entrepreneurial experiments. Friends and acquaintances from his university days recall Musk as being exceptionally driven and focused, with a clear vision of his future and a deep-seated desire to change the world.

After completing his undergraduate degrees, Musk's initial plan was to pursue a PhD in energy physics/materials science at Stanford University in California, driven by a desire to work on technologies for sustainable energy. However, this plan was short-lived; Musk left Stanford after just two days, deciding instead to focus on entrepreneurial ventures that could have an immediate impact. This decision was made in the context of the internet boom of the 1990s—a period of rapid technological advancement and opportunity.

CHAPTER 2: THE FIRST VENTURES

The mid-to-late 1990s was a pivotal time in the technology industry, marked by the rapid expansion of the internet and the birth of numerous startups that would go on to become giants in the industry. Musk recognized the potential of the internet to change how people lived and worked. He believed that the opportunities presented by the burgeoning internet economy were too significant to pass up, and that delaying his entry into the business world to pursue further academic studies could mean missing out on these opportunities.

Zip2

The Internet, once a fledgling network of interconnected computers, was beginning to transform into the vast, indispensable global infrastructure we know today. It was against this backdrop of technological ferment that Elon Musk embarked on his first major entrepreneurial venture, Zip2 Corporation. This early foray into the business world would lay the groundwork for Musk's future endeavors and shape his approach to innovation and entrepreneurship.

After leaving Stanford University's PhD program in energy physics/materials science just two days in, Elon Musk, along with his brother, Kimbal Musk, saw an opportunity in the burgeoning Internet sector. In 1995, they founded Global

Link Information Network, which would later be renamed Zip2 Corporation. The company aimed to provide online business directories and maps for newspapers, a novel concept at the time that combined the utility of traditional Yellow Pages with the nascent technology of the Internet.

Starting with a modest setup, the Musk brothers ran the company out of a small, rented office in Palo Alto, California — the heart of Silicon Valley. The early days of Zip2 were a testament to the Musk brothers' determination and resourcefulness. With a small team, limited resources, and Elon Musk himself coding much of the company's initial software, Zip2 sought to carve out its niche by offering a valuable service to businesses and consumers alike.

The road to success for Zip2 was not without its challenges. The company initially struggled to convince businesses and newspapers of the value of an online presence. During these early stages, Elon Musk demonstrated his relentless work ethic and vision, often sleeping in the office and showering at the local YMCA, as recounted in various interviews. Despite these hurdles, the Musk brothers' persistence began to pay off as more and more businesses started to recognize the potential of the Internet for reaching customers.

Zip2 evolved to provide not just business directories and maps, but also city guides for newspapers, allowing them to offer their readers an online service that included entertainment listings, local business services, and directions. This evolution of the company's services demonstrated Musk's ability to adapt and respond to the needs of the market, a trait that would become a hallmark of his approach to business.

Zip2's growing success caught the attention of the larger tech industry, and in 1999, Compaq Computer Corporation acquired Zip2 for approximately $307 million in cash. This acquisition was one of the largest deals in the Internet sector at the time and marked a significant milestone in Elon Musk's career. Musk's share from the sale amounted to $22 million, a substantial sum that would enable him to pursue further entrepreneurial ventures.

X.com

After the successful sale of Zip2, Elon Musk was not one to rest on his laurels. With the internet still in its nascent stages of transforming global commerce, Musk identified another sector ripe for innovation: financial services. In 1999, leveraging the capital he gained from the Zip2 sale, Musk embarked on a venture that would eventually revolutionize the way money is exchanged online. This new venture was X.com, an online payment and financial services company.

X.com was founded in March 1999, at a time when the idea of conducting financial transactions over the internet was still novel and fraught with skepticism. The vision behind X.com was bold and ambitious: to create a global payment system that was instant, secure, and universally accessible. Musk envisioned a world where financial transactions could be as simple and seamless as sending an email.

The inception of X.com was a direct response to the complexities and inefficiencies of traditional banking. Musk aimed to leverage the power of the internet to simplify financial services, making them more user-friendly and accessible to the general public. This vision was not just about disrupting the financial industry; it was about democratizing access to financial services.

X.com's journey was met with significant challenges from the outset. One of the most pressing issues was building trust with consumers. The idea of online banking and transferring money electronically was still new, and convincing users to adopt this technology required overcoming considerable skepticism regarding security and reliability.

Moreover, the regulatory landscape for online financial services was complex. Navigating this environment required careful planning and compliance to ensure that X.com operated within the legal frameworks of the jurisdictions in which it operated. Musk and his team had to invest considerable time and resources into ensuring that their service met these regulatory requirements, all while striving to maintain the simplicity and user-friendliness of their platform.

Despite these hurdles, X.com experienced rapid growth, attracting significant interest from investors and customers alike. Its user-friendly interface, combined with the novelty and convenience of its services, helped it quickly gain a foothold in the online payments market.

X.com's trajectory took a significant turn in 2000, when it merged with Confinity, a software company best known for its money-transfer service, PayPal. The merger was driven by the complementary nature of the two companies' services and the recognition that a unified platform could offer a more robust and comprehensive service to customers.

Initially, there was internal debate about the direction of the newly merged company, including disagreements over business strategies and the technology platform that should be used. Musk was a strong advocate for focusing on the X.com brand and its financial services, but others in the company saw the PayPal money transfer service as the more promising path forward.

Musk was ousted from his CEO position while on his honeymoon, and the company was renamed PayPal in 2001, reflecting a strategic shift to focus exclusively on the money transfer service. This decision proved to be pivotal. PayPal quickly became synonymous with online payments, growing at an exponential rate.

In 2002, PayPal was acquired by eBay for $1.5 billion in stock, just a few years after X.com was founded. This acquisition marked the culmination of Musk's vision for a revolutionized financial sector. Though Musk had faced challenges, including being ousted from the company, PayPal's success validated his belief in the potential of internet-based services to transform traditional industries.

Elon Musk, who was PayPal's largest shareholder after the company was formed through the merger of X.com and Confinity, owned 11.7% of PayPal's shares. Based on the acquisition terms and his ownership percentage, Musk's share from the sale amounted to approximately $175 million. This significant financial windfall from the PayPal sale provided Musk with the capital necessary to fund his next set of ambitious ventures, including SpaceX, Tesla, and later, SolarCity, thereby laying the foundation for his future successes in the technology and aerospace industries.

CHAPTER 3: TESLA MOTORS

Elon Musk's foray into the electric vehicle industry was driven by his long-standing conviction that the reliance on fossil fuels was unsustainable. He envisioned a future where transportation was powered by renewable energy, primarily electric vehicles, which he believed could be both efficient and desirable. However, the electric vehicles of the early 2000s were far from appealing to the general public, often criticized for their lackluster performance and limited range.

Tesla Motors was founded in 2003 by Martin Eberhard and Marc Tarpenning, but it was Musk's involvement and vision that catapulted the company into the spotlight. Musk became involved with Tesla in February 2004, leading the company's initial round of investment funding and joining the board of directors as chairman. Although not a founder, his early and significant involvement, combined with his strategic vision and financial support, quickly made him a central figure in the company's development.

Early Challenges

Tesla's journey was fraught with challenges from the outset. The high cost of batteries, skepticism about the viability of EVs, and the Herculean task of establishing a new automobile company in a market dominated by century-old giants posed significant hurdles.

Financial Struggles: The financial aspect was among the most daunting challenges Tesla faced. Building a car company from the ground up is an enormously expensive venture, especially for a company like Tesla, which aimed to disrupt the automotive industry with high-cost, cutting-edge technology. The initial development and production of the Tesla Roadster required significant capital, and the company struggled to maintain financial stability, coming close to bankruptcy in 2 008.

Elon Musk's personal commitment played a crucial role in overcoming Tesla's financial struggles. He invested a significant portion of his own fortune into the company during its critical phases, showcasing his belief in Tesla's mission. This not only provided the necessary capital to keep the company afloat but also helped attract additional investments. Strategic partnerships with Daimler AG and Toyota brought in crucial funds and credibility, helping Tesla stabilize financially and continue its operations.

Technical Hurdles: The development of a reliable and high-performance electric powertrain was another significant hurdle. The market for electric vehicles (EVs) was virtually non-existent due to past failures to deliver on range and performance. The Roadster needed to break this stereotype by proving that EVs could compete with traditional sports cars in every respect.

Tesla invested heavily in research and development to innovate and refine its electric powertrain technology. The company's breakthrough came with the development of the Roadster, which could accelerate from 0 to 60 mph in less than 4 seconds and had a range of over 200 miles on a single charge. Tesla's approach included the use of lithium-ion battery cells, similar to those found in laptops, configured in a novel way to enhance performance and safety. This not only set new standards for electric vehicles but also demonstrated Tesla's technical prowess and innovation capability.

Market Skepticism: Overcoming market skepticism was perhaps one of the most intangible yet pervasive challenges. The prevailing view was that electric cars were inferior to gasoline-powered vehicles in terms of performance, range, and convenience. Changing this perception required Tesla not only to build an exceptional product but also to alter deeply ingrained consumer beliefs.

Tesla addressed this challenge by focusing on creating products that were superior in performance, safety, and environmental impact. The Roadster, and later the Model S, served as flagship examples of what electric vehicles could achieve, challenging and changing public perceptions. Moreover, Tesla adopted a unique marketing strategy that leveraged high-profile endorsements and media coverage, coupled with direct-to-consumer sales through stores and galleries, to educate the public and build a strong brand around sustainability and innovation.

Resistance from Traditional Auto Industry: Tesla's innovative direct sales model and its push for electric vehicles faced resistance from the traditional automotive industry and dealership networks. The established auto industry was hesitant to embrace electric vehicles, and dealer associations lobbied against Tesla's sales model, which bypassed traditional dealerships.

Tesla fought legal battles to defend its right to sell directly to consumers in various states, arguing that this model was essential for educating consumers about electric vehicles and providing the best customer experience. This persistence paid off, allowing Tesla to maintain control over its sales process and customer interactions. Additionally, Tesla's success and the growing public interest in electric vehicles gradually led to a shift in the industry's stance towards EVs, with more traditional automakers beginning to explore and invest in electric vehicle technology.

The Different Models

Tesla's lineup of electric vehicles (EVs) has grown to include several models, each designed with unique features to cater to different segments of the market. Tesla's vehicles are renowned for their performance, cutting-edge technology, and environmental benefits.

Tesla Roadster

The original Tesla Roadster holds a special place in the history of electric vehicles as Tesla's first production car, representing a significant milestone in the company's mission to accelerate the world's transition to sustainable energy. Here's an overview of the Roadster, covering its release, features, price, sales performance, and public reception.

The Tesla Roadster was officially released in 2008. It was the first highway-legal electric vehicle to use lithium-ion battery cells and the first electric vehicle to travel over 200 miles per charge. The Roadster was a bold statement from the then-fledgling Tesla, showcasing its commitment to creating high-performance, attractive electric vehicles that could compete with traditional gasoline-powered sports cars.

The Tesla Roadster was built on a chassis shared with the Lotus Elise, but with significant modifications to accommodate its electric powertrain. Key features included:

Performance: The Roadster could accelerate from 0 to 60 mph in under 4 seconds, with a top speed of 125 mph, making it one of the fastest production electric vehicles at the time.

Range: It boasted an impressive range of over 240 miles on a single charge, a groundbreaking achievement that challenged prevailing perceptions about the viability of electric vehicles for long-distance travel.

Battery Technology: The Roadster used a lithium-ion battery pack, which was innovative for electric vehicles at the time and contributed to its high performance and range.

Design: With its sleek, sporty design, the Roadster appealed to sports car enthusiasts and environmentally conscious consumers alike. Its convertible top added to its appeal as a fun, stylish vehicle.

The original Tesla Roadster's base price was around $109,000, positioning it as a luxury sports car. The high price reflected its advanced technology, performance capabilities, and the costs associated with pioneering electric vehicle production.

The Tesla Roadster was produced in limited quantities, with about 2,450 units sold across over 30 countries by the time production ended in 2012. While these numbers may seem modest compared to mainstream vehicles, the Roadster was never intended to be a mass-market car. Instead, it served as a proof of concept and a statement of Tesla's ambitions in the electric vehicle market.

The Roadster received critical acclaim for its performance, range, and engineering, winning numerous awards and accolades. It played a crucial role in changing public perceptions about electric vehicles, demonstrating that they could be desirable, high-performance cars rather than just economical, utilitarian modes of transportation. The Roadster also helped establish Tesla's reputation as a leader in electric vehicle technology.

Critics praised the Roadster for its acceleration, handling, and the novelty of driving a fully electric sports car. However, some criticized its price, interior ergonomics, and comfort over long distances, noting that it was a first-generation product with room for improvement.

Tesla Model S

The Tesla Model S was officially launched in June 2012. It was Tesla's second vehicle model after the Roadster and its first electric sedan. The Model S was designed to be a high-performance electric vehicle from the ground up, unlike the Roadster, which was based on the Lotus Elise chassis. This approach allowed for greater innovation in vehicle design, battery technology, and performance.

From its inception, the Model S has been notable for several groundbreaking features and continual improvements through both hardware upgrades and over-the-air software updates. Key features have included:

Performance: Various iterations of the Model S have offered impressive acceleration, with certain versions capable of going from 0 to 60 mph in just over 2 seconds. This performance is facilitated by Tesla's powerful electric motors and innovative battery technology.

Range: At its introduction, the Model S set new standards for electric vehicle range. Over the years, through improvements in battery technology, some versions of the Model S have achieved ranges of over 400 miles on a single charge, according to EPA estimates.

Autopilot: The Model S was among the first vehicles to offer Tesla's Autopilot, an advanced driver-assistance system capable of handling some driving tasks, with periodic updates increasing its capabilities.

Interior and Technology: The interior of the Model S is dominated by a large touchscreen interface that controls most of the car's functions, from navigation to climate control. The vehicle has been praised for its minimalist interior design, spaciousness, and technological features.

Safety: The Model S has consistently achieved high safety ratings from various organizations, benefiting from the inherent safety advantages of its electric architecture and Tesla's focus on safety in design.

At launch, the base price of the Model S was around $57,400 for the 40 kWh battery version, before federal tax incentives for electric vehicles. Over the years, as Tesla introduced versions with larger batteries, more features, and higher performance, the price of the Model S has increased. The more recent high-performance variants, such as the Plaid model, have been priced significantly higher, reflecting their advanced technology and capabilities.

The Tesla Model S has been a commercial success, with sales increasing steadily over the years. It quickly became the best-selling electric car in several countries shortly after its release and has continued to hold a significant share of the luxury car market.

The public and critics alike have widely praised the Model S. It has been lauded for its innovative use of technology, impressive performance, and driving range, setting it apart from other vehicles in the electric vehicle market. The Model S has won numerous awards, including Motor Trend's 2013 Car of the Year, and has set benchmarks for what consumers can expect from an electric vehicle.

Tesla Model X

The Tesla Model X was officially released in September 2015, after several delays that increased anticipation for the vehicle. The Model X was developed to cater to the growing demand for family-friendly electric vehicles, offering more space and versatility than the Model S sedan.

The Model X is distinguished by several innovative features that set it apart from both conventional and electric SUVs:

Falcon Wing Doors: Perhaps the most visually striking feature of the Model X is its rear falcon-wing doors, which open upwards instead of outwards. This design allows for easier access to the second and third-row seats, even in tight parking spaces.

Performance: Like other Tesla vehicles, the Model X offers impressive acceleration, with certain configurations capable of going from 0 to 60 mph in as little as 2.7 seconds. This performance is matched with all-wheel drive as standard, enhancing its capabilities in various driving conditions.

Safety: The Model X has been noted for its safety features, including a low center of gravity that reduces the risk of rollover, a reinforced structure to protect occupants, and standard active safety features. It has received high safety ratings from various organizations.

Autopilot and Full Self-Driving Capability: The Model X comes with Autopilot, Tesla's advanced driver-assistance system, and has the option for full self-driving capability in the future through over-the-air software updates.

Range: At its launch, the Model X already offered a competitive electric range, which has improved in newer models through advancements in battery technology. The latest versions can achieve ranges of over 300 miles on a single charge, according to EPA estimates.

Interior: The Model X's interior is designed for comfort and functionality, offering seating for up to seven adults and a panoramic windshield that extends overhead for a spacious feel.

At launch, the Model X's price started at around $80,000 for the base model, with higher-performance versions and additional features increasing the price significantly. The price reflects the Model X's position in the market as a luxury electric SUV with advanced technology and performance capabilities.

The Model X has sold well since its launch, contributing significantly to Tesla's overall sales figures, although it has generally sold in lower volumes than the

Model S and Model 3. Its unique features, particularly the falcon-wing doors, have been a point of fascination and differentiation in the market.

Public and critical reception of the Model X has been largely positive, with praise for its performance, safety features, and environmental benefits. However, the Model X has also faced criticism, primarily for its high price point, the complexity and reliability of its falcon-wing doors, and initial quality issues in early production models. Over time, Tesla has addressed many of these concerns through improvements in manufacturing and quality control.

Tesla Model 3

The Tesla Model 3 was officially unveiled in March 2016, with deliveries beginning in July 2017. It represented Tesla's first foray into a more mass-market segment of electric vehicles, following the success of its more premium models, the Model S and Model X.

The Model 3 is known for several key features that have contributed to its popularity:

Performance: The Model 3 offers impressive acceleration, with certain variants capable of going from 0 to 60 mph in just over 3 seconds. It balances performance with efficiency, providing a thrilling driving experience along with long range and low operating costs.

Range: One of the standout features of the Model 3 is its range. The standard range version offers a considerable driving range on a single charge, which has been further extended in the Long Range and Performance versions, making it practical for both daily use and longer trips.

Autopilot: Like other Tesla vehicles, the Model 3 comes with Autopilot capabilities, Tesla's advanced driver-assistance system, which offers features such as adaptive cruise control and lane-keeping assistance. Full Self-Driving capability is available as an optional upgrade, promising more advanced autonomous driving features in the future through over-the-air software updates.

Interior and Technology: The Model 3's interior is minimalist and centered around a large touchscreen that controls most of the car's functions, from navigation to climate control. The vehicle includes Tesla's latest technology and safety features, contributing to its high safety ratings.

Supercharging: Access to Tesla's Supercharger network enables quick recharging during longer trips, enhancing the Model 3's practicality and appeal as a primary vehicle for a wide range of consumers.

At its unveiling, the base price of the Model 3 was announced to be $35,000 before any federal or state incentives, making it significantly more accessible than the Model S or Model X. Over time, changes in production, the introduction of different variants, and adjustments in Tesla's pricing strategy have influenced the Model 3's price, with higher-end versions costing more due to additional features and performance capabilities.

The Model 3 has been a commercial success, quickly becoming one of the world's best-selling electric vehicles. Its combination of affordability, performance, safety, and access to Tesla's ecosystem (including the Supercharger network) has made it extremely popular among consumers. The Model 3 has significantly contributed to Tesla's overall sales volume and has played a crucial role in increasing the adoption of electric vehicles globally.

The public and critical reception of the Model 3 has been overwhelmingly positive. Consumers and reviewers alike have praised its driving performance, range, safety features, and the value it offers as an electric vehicle. The Model 3 has won numerous awards and accolades, further cementing its position as a landmark vehicle in the EV market.

Tesla Model Y

The Tesla Model Y is an all-electric compact SUV that builds on the technologies and successes of its predecessors, particularly the Model 3, from which it borrows much of its architecture. The Model Y was designed to cater to a broader market by combining the affordability and performance of the Model 3 with the versatility and space of an SUV.

The Tesla Model Y was unveiled in March 2019, with initial deliveries beginning in March 2020. The introduction of the Model Y was part of Tesla's ongoing strategy to expand its electric vehicle lineup to include more accessible and family-friendly options.

The Model Y includes several notable features that have contributed to its appeal:

Performance and Range: The Model Y offers impressive performance, with acceleration from 0 to 60 mph in as little as 3.5 seconds for the Performance model. It also boasts a remarkable electric range, with some variants capable of traveling over 300 miles on a single charge, making it one of the most efficient vehicles in its class.

Versatility and Space: Designed as a compact SUV, the Model Y provides ample interior space with seating for up to seven passengers with an optional third row. It also offers generous cargo space, enhanced by a front trunk (frunk) and foldable rear seats.

Autopilot and Full Self-Driving Capability: Similar to other Tesla vehicles, the Model Y comes equipped with Autopilot features, and it offers the potential for full self-driving capabilities in the future through over-the-air software updates.

Safety: The Model Y has been designed with safety as a priority, incorporating Tesla's latest active safety technologies, structural integrity, and a low center of gravity to minimize the risk of rollover.

Interior Design: The interior of the Model Y follows Tesla's minimalist design philosophy, with a large central touchscreen serving as the hub for most of the car's controls and functions. The all-glass roof provides an open, airy feel to the cabin.

At its launch, the pricing for the Model Y started at around $39,000 for the Standard Range version, making it more affordable than the Model X but slightly higher in price than the Model 3. Over time, Tesla has adjusted the Model Y's pricing and available configurations, discontinuing some options while introducing others, such as the Long Range and Performance models. Prices vary based on the chosen configuration, optional features, and potential changes in Tesla's pricing strategy.

The Tesla Model Y has enjoyed strong sales since its release, quickly becoming one of Tesla's best-selling models. Its combination of SUV versatility, electric efficiency, performance, and advanced technology has made it extremely popular among consumers, contributing significantly to Tesla's overall sales volumes.

The public and critical reception of the Model Y has been largely positive, with praise for its performance, range, interior space, and the value it offers as a compact electric SUV. It has been recognized as a compelling option for families and individuals seeking an all-electric vehicle that doesn't compromise on space, comfort, or driving enjoyment.

Tesla Semi

The Tesla Semi was unveiled in November 2017, with initial production and deliveries initially projected to start in 2019. However, the production has faced delays, and as of December 2023, only around 100 Tesla Semis have been delivered, primarily to PepsiCo.

The Tesla Semi boasts several impressive features aimed at improving the efficiency, safety, and cost-effectiveness of freight hauling:

Performance: The Tesla Semi is designed to be capable of accelerating from 0 to 60 mph in 20 seconds, even when fully loaded with 80,000 pounds, the maximum weight for U.S. highway freight trucks. This performance level is a stark contrast to traditional diesel trucks.

Range: Tesla announced two versions of the Semi, with estimated ranges of 300 miles and 500 miles on a single charge under full load conditions, addressing one of the most significant concerns about electric vehicles in long-haul trucking.

Charging: The Semi is expected to utilize Tesla's new Megachargers, a network of high-speed DC chargers. Tesla has claimed that these chargers could provide about 400 miles of range in 30 minutes.

Safety: The Semi includes Tesla's Enhanced Autopilot system, offering semi-autonomous capabilities such as automatic emergency braking, lane keeping, and lane departure warning. The design also places the driver in the center of the cab for enhanced visibility, and the vehicle's low center of gravity helps reduce the risk of rollover.

Cost Savings: Tesla has touted the Semi's potential for significant savings in fuel costs compared to diesel trucks, with estimated operating costs of $1.26 per mile for the Semi compared to $1.51 per mile for diesel trucks.

At its unveiling, the expected base prices for the Tesla Semi were announced as approximately $150,000 for the 300-mile range version and $180,000 for the 500-mile range version. These prices are subject to change based on production costs, configurations, and other factors by the time more significant production begins.

Given the delays in production and limited deliveries as of late 2023, it's difficult to gauge the Tesla Semi's sales performance conclusively. However, the announcement of the Semi was met with considerable interest from the logistics and transportation industry. However, Elon Musk has announced his aim to produce 50,000 Tesla Semis in 2024.

Tesla Roadster (2nd Generation)

The new Roadster was unveiled by Elon Musk in November 2017 as a prototype, with initial expectations for production to start in 2020. However, production has faced delays. Currently, the 2nd Generation Tesla Roadster is due to be released in 2026 and can currently be reserved for a deposit of $50,000.

Despite not yet being available for purchase, the second-generation Tesla Roadster has generated significant excitement based on its announced features, which aim to set new benchmarks for electric vehicle performance:

Performance: The new Roadster promises record-breaking performance figures, including a 0-60 mph acceleration time of 1.9 seconds, making it one of the fastest cars in the world. It's also expected to achieve a top speed of over 250 mph and complete a quarter mile in under 9 seconds.

Range: Elon Musk announced an estimated range of over 620 miles on a single charge, thanks to a 200 kWh battery pack. This would be the highest range of any electric vehicle announced to date, significantly extending the practicality and appeal of electric sports cars.

All-Wheel Drive: The Roadster is expected to feature all-wheel drive, with electric motors powering both the front and rear wheels, enhancing its performance and handling capabilities.

Seating: Unlike many high-performance sports cars, the new Roadster is designed with four seats, though the rear seats are expected to be relatively small, making them more suitable for occasional use or small passengers.

The base price for the new Tesla Roadster is expected to start at $200,000, with the first 1,000 units being a special "Founders Series" priced at $250,000.

Tesla Cybertruck

Unveiled in November 2019 by Elon Musk, the Cybertruck's design, performance, and features immediately captured public attention, sparking a wide range of reactions due to its unconventional aesthetics and ambitious specifications. The Tesla Cybertruck is designed to offer the utility and ruggedness of a traditional pickup truck, combined with the performance and environmental benefits of an electric vehicle. Key announced features include:

Design: One of the most striking aspects of the Cybertruck is its design, featuring a distinctive angular, futuristic exterior made from a stainless steel exoskeleton. This material, called Ultra-Hard 30X Cold-Rolled stainless steel, is touted for its durability and resistance to dents, damage, and corrosion.

Performance: The Cybertruck promises impressive performance, with the top-of-the-line model capable of accelerating from 0 to 60 mph in approximately 2.9 seconds. It also boasts remarkable towing capacity and off-road capabilities.

Range: Tesla announced three versions of the Cybertruck, with estimated ranges starting at 250+ miles for the single motor rear-wheel-drive version, 300+ miles for the dual-motor all-wheel-drive version, and up to 500+ miles for the tri-motor all-wheel-drive version.

Utility: The Cybertruck is designed with functionality in mind, featuring a 6.5-foot cargo bed (dubbed the "Cybertruck Vault"), a versatile adaptive air suspension system, and a spacious interior with seating for up to six adults.

Autopilot: Like other Tesla vehicles, the Cybertruck comes equipped with Tesla's Autopilot advanced driver-assistance system, with the potential for full self-driving capabilities in the future through software updates.

At its unveiling, Tesla announced the following starting prices for the Cybertruck, which varied based on the number of motors and corresponding performance capabilities:

Single Motor RWD: starting at $39,900

Dual Motor AWD: starting at $49,900

Tri-Motor AWD: starting at $69,900

However, despite these announced prices, due to high inflation over the pandemic, the prices have been increased significantly, with the base model beginning at a price of $60,990.

The unveiling of the Cybertruck generated significant media attention and public discussion, largely due to its unconventional design and ambitious performance claims. The reception was mixed, with some praising its innovative approach and potential to revolutionize the pickup truck market, while others were skeptical or critical of its design and feasibility.

Despite the mixed initial reactions, the Cybertruck received a substantial number of reservations within days of its unveiling, indicating strong interest from a segment of consumers excited by Tesla's vision for the future of electric utility vehicles. Deliveries only began in late November 2023, and the Cybertruck is currently only available in North America.

CHAPTER 4: SPACEX

Elon Musk founded SpaceX in March 2002, after PayPal was purchased by eBay for $1.5 billion. Musk's interest in space was not new; it was part of a broader vision that included the internet, clean energy, and space as the domains where he wanted to drive significant change.

In the early 2000s, Elon Musk was looking for ways to reduce the cost of space travel with the ultimate goal of colonizing Mars. One of his initial ideas was to purchase intercontinental ballistic missiles (ICBMs) without warheads from Russia, which he could then repurpose to send payloads into space. This approach was motivated by the high costs of rockets available in the United States and Musk's belief that a dramatic reduction in launch costs was necessary to advance space exploration.

Musk made two trips to Russia, in 2001 and 2002, with Jim Cantrell, an aerospace supplies fixer, and Mike Griffin, who had worked for the CIA's venture capital arm, In-Q-Tel. Musk's intention was to buy refurbished ICBMs from the Russians. During these visits, he met with several Russian aerospace companies and attempted to negotiate a deal to purchase the rockets.

However, the negotiations proved to be challenging. The Russian aerospace manufacturers were not convinced of Musk's seriousness and commitment to the project. On the first trip, they largely ignored his proposals. On the second trip, they quoted him a price of $8 million per rocket, which Musk found exorbitantly high and not at all in line with his goal of making space travel more affordable.

Frustrated by the lack of progress and the dismissive attitude he encountered in Russia, Musk had an epiphany on the flight back to the United States. He realized that the cost of the raw materials for building a rocket was only a small fraction of the sales price of a finished rocket. This disparity suggested that there was significant room for reducing costs through innovation in the production process and supply chain management.

Determined to find a more affordable way to achieve his space ambitions, Musk decided to start his own rocket company. He believed that by applying vertical integration, leveraging commercially available technology, and designing rockets for reusability, he could dramatically reduce the cost of space travel.

This realization led to the founding of SpaceX in 2002. Musk's initial plan was to develop the Falcon 1, a small, relatively inexpensive rocket that could carry satellites to orbit.

Early Challenges

SpaceX's early days were fraught with challenges. The aerospace industry was dominated by government agencies like NASA and large, established defense contractors with deep pockets and decades of experience. The cost of launching a rocket was astronomical, largely due to the traditional reliance on single-use launch vehicles. Moreover, the technology for reusable rockets, which Musk identified as key to reducing costs, was unproven and considered risky by industry standards.

In addition to technical and financial hurdles, SpaceX also faced regulatory and logistical challenges. Gaining access to launch sites, obtaining the necessary government permissions, and navigating the complex web of international space treaties added layers of complexity to SpaceX's operational challenges.

Despite these obstacles, Musk was undeterred. He invested a significant portion of his fortune into SpaceX, determined to build the company from the ground up. The early team at SpaceX was a mix of young engineers and industry veterans, all united by the mission to drastically reduce space launch costs and enable Mars colonization. This team's dedication and Musk's leadership would soon begin to reshape the landscape of space exploration.

The Falcon 1 Milestone

After Elon Musk founded SpaceX in 2002, the company set out to design the Falcon 1, a small, cost-effective rocket capable of carrying payloads to orbit. The design aimed to minimize complexity and cost, using a single Merlin engine in its first stage and a simpler pressure-fed Kestrel engine in its second stage. The Falcon 1 was designed to be partially reusable, with plans to recover the first stage for refurbishment and reuse.

SpaceX faced a steep learning curve, as the company had to develop its own engines, avionics, and materials from scratch. The development of the Merlin engine, in particular, was a significant technical challenge. The team conducted extensive testing, including static fire tests of the engines and stages to validate their performance and reliability. The Falcon 1 was manufactured at SpaceX's facilities in Hawthorne, California. The company adopted a vertical integration approach, producing the majority of the rocket's components in-house to reduce costs and maintain quality control. Once manufactured, the components were assembled and integrated into a complete rocket, ready for launch.

On March 24, 2006, the inaugural flight of the Falcon 1 ended in failure just 33 seconds after liftoff. The cause was traced to a fuel leak and subsequent fire around the Merlin engine's base, which led to the loss of control and disintegration of the vehicle. This failure highlighted the complexities of rocket engineering and the challenges of developing new launch vehicles.

On March 21, 2007, the second flight of the Falcon 1 also ended in failure. The rocket successfully reached space; however, a problem occurred during stage separation. The second stage engine igniter failed to start, and the vehicle did not reach orbit. The failure was attributed to a design issue that allowed the stages to bump into each other during separation.

On August 2, 2008, the third launch attempt of the Falcon 1 again ended in failure. The rocket's first stage performed nominally, but the second stage experienced a residual thrust that prevented it from reaching orbit. The failure was caused by a design flaw in the separation system and an incorrect configuration of the flight computer.

Finally, on September 28, 2008, the Falcon 1 successfully reached orbit on its fourth attempt, becoming the first privately developed liquid-fueled rocket to do so. This historic achievement validated SpaceX's approach and technologies, proving that the company could overcome setbacks and deliver on its promises.

Rockets and Spacecraft

Following the Falcon 1, SpaceX has developed a series of more powerful and advanced rockets and spacecraft:

Falcon 9: SpaceX's workhorse rocket, capable of carrying cargo and crew to orbit. The first successful launch occurred on June 4, 2010. Its design includes a reusable first stage, a breakthrough that has significantly reduced the cost of access to space.

Falcon Heavy: The most powerful operational rocket in the world as of its first flight in February 2018. It's designed for heavy payloads, capable of carrying large satellites, spacecraft, and potential missions to the Moon or Mars.

Dragon: A spacecraft designed to deliver cargo (Cargo Dragon) and crew (Crew Dragon) to the International Space Station (ISS). The first successful cargo mission occurred in May 2012, and the first crewed mission, Demo-2, launched successfully on May 30, 2020.

Starship: The next-generation spacecraft currently under development, intended for missions to the Moon, Mars, and beyond. Starship aims to be fully reusable and capable of carrying up to 100 people.

Successful Missions and Achievements

SpaceX's successful missions have included a number of significant "firsts" and achievements:

Commercial Cargo and Crew to the ISS: SpaceX became the first private company to send a spacecraft (Dragon) to the ISS in 2012 and to send astronauts there in 2020.

Reusability: SpaceX has successfully landed the Falcon 9's first stage multiple times on both land and autonomous spaceport drone ships, dramatically reducing launch costs and increasing the frequency of launches.

Starlink: SpaceX has deployed thousands of small satellites as part of its Starlink project, aimed at providing global high-speed internet. The project represents one of the largest satellite constellations ever deployed.

Falcon Heavy's Debut: The maiden flight of the Falcon Heavy included sending Musk's personal Tesla Roadster into an orbit around the Sun, demonstrating the rocket's capability in a unique way.

SpaceX's successes have positioned it as a leader in the aerospace industry, securing contracts with NASA, the U.S. Department of Defense, and numerous commercial clients. Its achievements in reusability have lowered costs and increased the accessibility of space. Furthermore, the company's valuation has soared, reflecting its success in attracting investment and its potential for future growth.

Challenges

Despite its successes, SpaceX has faced challenges, including:

Launch Failures: Like any aerospace company, SpaceX has experienced setbacks, including failed launches and explosions during testing. Each failure has been met with a rigorous review process, leading to improvements in design and operations.

Development Delays: High-profile projects like the Falcon Heavy and Crew Dragon have experienced delays, a common challenge in the aerospace industry given the complexity of developing new space technologies.

Regulatory and Environmental Concerns: SpaceX's increased launch cadence and the development of Starlink have raised regulatory and environmental questions, including concerns about space traffic management and the impact of satellite constellations on astronomy.

CHAPTER 5: NEURALINK

The genesis of Neuralink is deeply entwined with Elon Musk's overarching concern for the future of humanity, particularly in the context of artificial intelligence (AI) and human cognition. Musk's decision to launch Neuralink in 2016 officially unveiled in March 2017, was not an isolated endeavor but rather a continuation of his life's work aimed at tackling what he perceives to be existential threats to humanity and exploring ways to ensure a prosperous future.

At the heart of Neuralink's inception lies Elon Musk's contemplation of the trajectory of artificial intelligence. Musk has been vocal about the potential perils associated with the advent of superintelligent AI systems, expressing concerns that humanity could be outpaced or even endangered by AI that evolves beyond human control or understanding. This perspective has been a significant driving force behind Musk's ventures, with Neuralink serving as a direct response to the challenge of integrating human consciousness with computational intelligence. By enhancing human cognitive capabilities through a brain-computer interface (BCI), Musk envisions creating a future where humans are not obsolete but instead become integral components of the AI landscape, thus mitigating the existential risks associated with autonomous AI.

Objectives

Neuralink's ambitious objectives reflect Elon Musk's vision of leveraging cutting-edge technology to expand human capabilities and address some of the most challenging medical conditions. Central to its mission are two interrelated goals: developing a high-bandwidth brain-machine interface (BMI) and using this technology to treat neurological conditions.

The quest to create a high-bandwidth BMI is rooted in the desire to enhance human cognitive abilities and provide a direct communication pathway between the brain and external devices, including computers and, eventually, artificial intelligence systems. This objective is motivated by several key considerations:

Enhancing Human Cognition: By establishing a seamless interface between the brain and digital systems, Neuralink aims to augment human cognitive capabilities, including memory, processing speed, and access to information. This could fundamentally alter how humans interact with technology, making the exchange of complex ideas instantaneous and intuitive.

Symbiosis with AI: Musk's vision of achieving a symbiotic relationship with artificial intelligence is central to Neuralink's mission. By integrating human consciousness with AI through a BMI, the company seeks to ensure that humans remain an integral part of the evolutionary trajectory of intelligence, rather than being sidelined by autonomous AI systems.

Overcoming Limitations of Current Interfaces: Existing interfaces between humans and computers, such as keyboards, mice, and touchscreens, are limited in bandwidth and efficiency. Neuralink's high-bandwidth BMI aims to overcome these limitations, facilitating a more natural and efficient flow of information between humans and machines.

To achieve this high-bandwidth connection, Neuralink is developing advanced microfabricated electrode arrays capable of recording and stimulating brain activity with unprecedented precision and minimal invasiveness. This involves overcoming significant engineering, neurological, and bio-compatibility challenges.

Beyond the futuristic vision of human-AI symbiosis, Neuralink is deeply committed to applying its BMI technology to treat and alleviate neurological conditions, offering new hope to those affected by various disorders:

Restoring Sensory and Motor Function: For individuals with spinal cord injuries, brain-machine interfaces hold the promise of bypassing damaged pathways, potentially restoring movement and sensation. By directly translating neural activity into control signals for assistive devices or even stimulating muscles, Neuralink aims to offer groundbreaking treatments for paralysis and motor dysfunction.

Treating Neurodegenerative Diseases: Diseases such as Parkinson's and Alzheimer's pose significant challenges to patients, families, and healthcare systems worldwide. Neuralink's technology could offer novel therapeutic approaches by stimulating specific brain regions, modulating neural activity, and potentially slowing disease progression or alleviating symptoms.

Mental Health and Beyond: The potential applications of Neuralink's technology extend into treating psychiatric disorders, including depression and anxiety, by targeting neural circuits involved in these conditions. The precise mechanisms and therapeutic protocols are areas of ongoing research and development.

Achievements and Progress

Since its inception, Neuralink has made significant strides in developing its brain-machine interface technology. Some of the notable achievements include:

Development of the "Link": The "Link" is a sophisticated neural implant device, which is designed to be implanted in the brain by a robotic surgeon. The device features flexible threads, thinner than a human hair, which can be inserted into the brain to monitor neural activity and potentially stimulate neural pathways.

Successful animal trials: Neuralink has demonstrated the functionality of its technology through experiments with animals. Notably, in August 2020, Neuralink showcased a live pig with a Link device implanted in its brain, demonstrating the device's ability to record neural activity in real-time. Further demonstrations involved showing a monkey with a Neuralink implant successfully controlling a computer cursor with its brain.

First Human Trial: In early 2024, Neuralink has successfully conducted its first human trial. While not much information has yet been released, it is said that the recipient is recovering well and that initial results show promising neuron spike detection. Neuralink is currently wanting to enlist people for trials aged 22 and above who are suffering with quadriplegia due to a spinal cord injury or myotrophic lateral sclerosis (ALS).

Challenges and Criticisms

Despite its groundbreaking aspirations, Neuralink has faced several challenges and criticisms, including:

Technical and Ethical Challenges: The development of safe, effective, and durable neural implants poses significant technical hurdles. Moreover, the prospect of brain-machine interfaces raises profound ethical questions concerning privacy, autonomy, and the potential for misuse.

Regulatory Hurdles: Given the invasive nature of Neuralink's proposed treatments, obtaining regulatory approval for human trials and eventual medical use is a complex and time-consuming process.

Skepticism from the Scientific Community: Some neuroscientists and ethicists have expressed skepticism about the feasibility of Neuralink's ambitious goals in the near term and have urged caution in managing public expectations.

Public and Scientific Reception

The public reception to Neuralink has been largely characterized by a sense of awe at the ambitious nature of its goals, combined with a healthy dose of skepticism regarding the feasibility and timeline of these advancements. The potential for enhancing human capabilities, treating neurological conditions, and even merging human consciousness with artificial intelligence captures the imagination, evoking scenarios often found in science fiction. Social media, tech forums, and comment sections on articles about Neuralink buzz with discussions about the implications of such technologies for the future of humanity.

However, this excitement is tempered by concerns over the ethical implications of brain-computer interfaces. Questions arise about privacy (who can access the data collected from a person's brain?), autonomy (could these devices influence behavior or decision-making?), and inequality (who will have access to these potentially expensive technologies?). The public is also wary of overpromising; the ambitious claims made by Neuralink have led some to adopt a "wait and see" attitude, especially given the complex nature of the human brain and the nascent stage of BMI technology.

The reception from the scientific and medical communities has been cautiously optimistic but also critical of the hype that sometimes surrounds Neuralink's announcements. Researchers and clinicians in neuroscience, neurosurgery, and neuroethics recognize the potential of Neuralink's technology to revolutionize the treatment of neurological disorders and enhance human capabilities. The prospect of high-bandwidth, minimally invasive BMIs could open new avenues for research and therapeutic interventions, potentially offering hope to millions suffering from conditions currently deemed untreatable.

However, experts have also raised concerns regarding the technical challenges, safety, and ethical considerations of implementing such technology. Neuralink's ambitious timeline and claims have been met with skepticism by some researchers who understand the complexities involved in translating laboratory findings into safe and effective clinical applications. The brain is an incredibly complex organ, and manipulating it without unintended consequences is a significant challenge.

Ethicists and neuroscientists alike have called for careful consideration of the implications of BMIs, emphasizing the need for robust ethical frameworks and regulations to guide the development and application of these technologies. The potential for misuse, privacy violations, and unforeseen side effects are topics of ongoing discussion within the academic community.

CHAPTER 6: SOLARCITY

SolarCity was a pivotal venture in Elon Musk's grand vision of a sustainable energy ecosystem. Founded in 2006 by Musk's cousins, Lyndon and Peter Rive, with Musk himself as the chairman and a primary investor, SolarCity grew to become one of the largest solar energy services companies in the United States. The company's mission was to reduce global dependence on fossil fuels by providing affordable, renewable solar energy to residential, commercial, and industrial customers.

The idea for SolarCity was influenced by Elon Musk's overarching concern for the environment and his belief in the necessity of transitioning to sustainable energy sources. Musk envisioned a three-pronged strategy, involving electric vehicles (Tesla), energy storage (Tesla Energy), and solar power (SolarCity). SolarCity was central to this vision, aiming to make solar energy accessible and affordable to a broader audience. The company offered end-to-end solar services, including design, financing, installation, monitoring, and maintenance of solar energy systems.

Products and Services

SolarCity focuses on some key products and services, namely:

Solar Panel Installation: Prior to the acquisition, of SolarCity by Tesla, So-larCity's core business was the design, financing, and installation of solar panel systems for homes, businesses, and government facilities. The company tailored solar solutions to fit the energy needs and financial situations of its customers, offering a clean, renewable energy source that could reduce electricity bills.

Solar Leasing and Power Purchase Agreements (PPAs): One of SolarCity's innovations was making solar energy more financially accessible through leasing and PPAs. Customers could lease solar panels or agree to a PPA, where they would pay for the electricity generated by the panels at a set price per kilowatt-hour, often lower than traditional utility rates. This model allowed customers to enjoy the benefits of solar energy with little to no upfront cost, removing a significant barrier to solar adoption.

Solar Roof: Although the Solar Roof became more closely associated with Tesla after the acquisition, it was part of SolarCity's vision for integrating solar technology into buildings aesthetically. The Solar Roof features solar cells integrated into glass roof tiles, creating a seamless, durable roof that generates electricity.

Energy Storage Solutions: Partnering with Tesla, SolarCity began offering energy storage solutions to complement its solar panel installations. The Tesla Powerwall, a rechargeable lithium-ion battery, allows homeowners to store excess solar energy generated during the day for use at night or during power outages, enhancing energy independence and reliability.

Energy Efficiency Evaluations and Upgrades: SolarCity also provided energy efficiency evaluations, recommending ways for customers to reduce energy consumption and improve their homes' overall energy efficiency. This service aimed to maximize the benefits of solar installation and contribute to broader efforts to reduce energy use and environmental impact.

Acquisition by Tesla

In August 2016, Tesla announced its intention to acquire SolarCity in a deal valued at approximately $2.6 billion. The acquisition was completed in November 2016, despite some initial skepticism from investors and analysts who were concerned about the financial health of SolarCity and potential conflicts of interest, given Musk's roles in both companies.

Tesla's acquisition of SolarCity was driven by several strategic objectives:

Integration into Tesla's Sustainable Energy Ecosystem: Musk aimed to create a seamless, integrated sustainable energy solution that combined electric vehicles, energy storage, and solar power. By acquiring SolarCity, Tesla could offer consumers a one-stop-shop for their energy needs, reinforcing its position as a leader in sustainable technology.

Expansion of Product Offerings: The acquisition allowed Tesla to broaden its product portfolio to include solar panels and the Solar Roof, an innovative product that integrates solar cells directly into roofing materials, making solar power more aesthetically pleasing and easier to adopt for homeowners.

Synergies with Energy Storage: SolarCity's solar energy solutions were complementary to Tesla's energy storage products, such as the Powerwall and Powerpack. Combining solar power generation with energy storage allowed Tesla to offer more comprehensive energy solutions that could provide clean energy around the clock, enhancing energy independence for consumers and businesses.

Plans and Vision for SolarCity within Tesla

Following the acquisition, Musk's vision for SolarCity was to integrate it into Tesla's broader mission to accelerate the world's transition to sustainable energy. Key aspects of this vision included:

Scaling Up Solar Deployment: Musk aimed to significantly increase the adoption of solar energy through innovative products like the Solar Roof and aggressive marketing and sales strategies. By leveraging Tesla's brand and retail presence, Musk believed SolarCity could reach a wider audience.

Innovation in Solar Technology: Continuing innovation in solar technology and energy storage was a priority, with the goal of making solar power more efficient, affordable, and appealing to consumers.

Energy Autonomy: A long-term goal of the acquisition was to enable consumers and communities to achieve energy autonomy, reducing reliance on traditional energy grids and fossil fuels. By combining solar panels, batteries, and electric vehicles, Tesla envisioned creating self-sustaining energy ecosystems for homes, businesses, and even entire communities.

CHAPTER 7: INNOVATIONS IN TRANSPORTATION

Elon Musk's vision for the future of transportation extends beyond electric vehicles and rockets. It encompasses a broader ambition to revolutionize how people move around the planet and reduce congestion within cities. Two of Musk's ventures, the Hyperloop and The Boring Company, reflect this ambition by proposing innovative solutions to age-old transportation challenges.

The Hyperloop

The Hyperloop is a proposed high-speed transportation system that seeks to revolutionize long-distance travel. Conceived by Elon Musk in a 2013 white paper, the Hyperloop concept involves transporting passengers and cargo in pods through a low-pressure tube at speeds that can exceed those of commercial air travel, potentially reaching up to 700 miles per hour. The system aims to be highly energy-efficient, weather-resistant, and faster than existing modes of mass transit, all while maintaining lower costs and environmental impact.

Musk introduced the Hyperloop concept as an alternative to California's high-speed rail project, which he criticized for its high costs and relatively slow speeds. Frustrated by the traffic in Los Angeles and the limitations of current transportation methods, Musk envisioned the Hyperloop as a "fifth mode of transport" — one that could provide rapid, on-demand travel between major cities with minimal energy usage and greenhouse gas emissions. While Musk himself did not initially pursue the development of the Hyperloop, he open-sourced the idea, encouraging entrepreneurs and engineers worldwide to take up the challenge.

The primary objective of the Hyperloop is to create a new transportation infrastructure that could dramatically reduce travel times between major urban centers, making it possible, for example, to commute between Los Angeles and San Francisco in about 30 minutes. Since Musk's initial proposal, several companies have been formed to realize the Hyperloop vision, including Virgin Hyperloop and Hyperloop Transportation Technologies (HTT).

These companies have focused on developing the technology and infrastructure required for the Hyperloop, such as the vacuum tubes, propulsion systems, and pod designs. While significant progress has been made, including successful tests of prototype pods and tracks, the Hyperloop concept is still in the developmental stage, with challenges related to safety, regulatory approval, and financing yet to be fully addressed.

The Boring Company

The Boring Company was founded by Elon Musk in late 2016 as a response to traffic congestion problems. It aims to decrease traffic in cities through the construction of a network of underground tunnels in which vehicles and high-speed trains can travel, bypassing surface congestion. The Boring Company's vision includes not just traditional tunneling projects but also innovative approaches to reducing costs and increasing the speed of tunnel construction.

Musk's frustration with Los Angeles traffic was the impetus behind The Boring Company. He mused about starting a company dedicated to boring and building tunnels to alleviate traffic, and thus The Boring Company was born. The company's vision extends beyond mere tunnel digging; it encompasses the creation of a multi-layered network of tunnels equipped with sleds that can transport cars at high speeds, effectively turning cars into a mass transit system.

The Boring Company's objectives include:

Reducing the cost and time of tunnel construction: The company aims to innovate in the tunneling process, making it faster and less expensive than current methods.

Developing the Loop system: A high-speed underground public transportation system in which passengers are transported on autonomous electric skates traveling at up to 150 miles per hour.

Creating infrastructure for the Hyperloop: While the Loop focuses on shorter distances within a city or region, The Boring Company also envisions its tunnels being used for the Hyperloop for longer intercity travel.

The Boring Company has launched several projects to demonstrate its technology and vision. Notable among these is the test tunnel in Hawthorne, California, near SpaceX's headquarters, which serves as a proof of concept for the company's tunneling and transportation ideas. The company has also proposed several other projects across the United States, including tunnels in Las Vegas, Chicago, and the Baltimore-Washington corridor, though not all have progressed to construction.

CHAPTER 8: PURCHASING TWITTER

The acquisition of Twitter (now "X") by Elon Musk marks a significant chapter in the narrative of one of the most influential tech entrepreneurs of the 21st century. Musk's interest in purchasing Twitter was driven by a complex mix of motivations related to free speech, platform governance, and the role of social media in public discourse.

Elon Musk's decision to purchase Twitter can be traced back to his vocal criticism of the platform's policies and his belief in the fundamental importance of free speech for democracy. Musk has been an active user of Twitter, utilizing the platform to communicate with the public, share updates on his various ventures, and occasionally stir controversy. His engagement with the platform highlighted both its potential and its pitfalls, leading him to contemplate more direct involvement.

In early 2022, Musk began acquiring shares of Twitter Inc., eventually becoming its largest individual shareholder. This move set the stage for a more ambitious proposal: purchasing the company outright and taking it private. Musk's offer to buy Twitter was motivated by his desire to implement changes he believed would unlock the platform's potential as a forum for free speech and debate, reduce the influence of algorithms on content visibility, and address issues related to moderation and censorship.

Musk's proposal to purchase Twitter was formalized in April 2022, with an offer valued at approximately $44 billion. After a period of negotiation, legal challenges, and considerable public and media scrutiny, the acquisition was completed in October 2022, marking one of the most high-profile tech acquisitions in recent history. On July 23rd 2023, Musk officially announced that Twitter would be rebranded as "X".

Following the acquisition, Musk initiated a series of changes aimed at reshaping Twitter (X) according to his vision. These changes have been wide-ranging, touching on aspects of the platform's operation, governance, and business model. Among the notable actions and proposals were:

Moderation and Free Speech: Musk expressed intentions to revise Twitter's content moderation policies to align more closely with his views on free speech, suggesting a more lenient approach to content that falls within the bounds of legality.

Platform Transparency: Musk advocated for greater transparency in Twitter's decision-making processes and the algorithms that determine content visibility, proposing open-sourcing parts of the platform's codebase.

Subscription Services: In an effort to diversify Twitter's revenue streams and reduce its reliance on advertising, Musk proposed the introduction of subscription services offering enhanced features for users.

Operational Overhaul: Musk's takeover was followed by significant operational changes, including layoffs as part of cost-cutting measures and restructuring efforts aimed at streamlining the platform's operations. Elon reportedly laid off 80% of Twitter staff, cutting it back to what he deemed to be only those who were essential to its successful operations.

The reception to Musk's acquisition of Twitter and the subsequent changes has been mixed. Supporters of Musk's vision have lauded the move as a necessary shake-up of the social media status quo, emphasizing the potential for positive

change in how the platform handles free speech, censorship, and user engagement. However, critics have raised concerns about the implications of Musk's
approach for misinformation, platform safety, and the overall impact on Twitter's
community and culture. The rapid pace of change has also led to uncertain-
ty among advertisers, users, and Twitter employees, with questions about the
long-term strategy and stability of the platform.

CHAPTER 9: MUSK'S PHILOSOPHY AND LEADERSHIP

Elon Musk is a figure who polarizes opinion like few others in the business world. His approach to entrepreneurship, leadership, and life is underpinned by a unique philosophy that has driven him to remarkable successes, while also drawing significant criticism. Understanding Musk's multifaceted persona requires delving into his guiding principles, leadership style, sources of success, and the critiques he has faced.

Musk's Philosophy

Solving Problems for Humanity: At the core of Musk's philosophy is a desire to address global challenges and enhance human life. Whether it's transitioning the world to sustainable energy, making human life multi-planetary, or integrating AI with human intelligence, his ventures often seek to solve problems that he perceives as critical to the future of humanity.

Perseverance Amidst Adversity: Musk is known for his resilience in the face of setbacks. His early career and the histories of SpaceX, Tesla, and his other companies are replete with examples of near-failures that were overcome through sheer perseverance. Musk's willingness to risk personal fortune for his companies' survival is testament to his commitment to his vision.

Thinking from First Principles: Musk advocates for reasoning from first principles rather than by analogy, a method derived from physics that involves breaking down complex problems into their most basic, fundamental truths and reasoning up from there. This approach allows him to re-imagine existing problems and devise innovative solutions.

Leadership Style

Visionary Leadership: Musk's ability to envision the future and inspire others with his vision is arguably his most potent leadership quality. His ambitious goals for companies like SpaceX and Tesla have not only attracted top talent but have also cultivated a culture of innovation and relentless pursuit of objectives.

Hands-On Approach: Musk is known for his detailed involvement in the operational and engineering aspects of his businesses. He often dives into the minutiae of product design, software code, and engineering problems, reflecting a leadership style that is both demanding and deeply involved.

Willingness to Take Risks: Musk's career has been characterized by high-stakes bets that many found imprudent or outright impossible. From investing his PayPal earnings into SpaceX and Tesla to purchasing Twitter, Musk's risk-taking is a hallmark of his leadership, driving innovation but also exposing his companies to significant challenges.

Successes in Business

Elon Musk's unprecedented success in business is deeply rooted in his unique combination of visionary thinking, relentless drive, and an unwavering belief in the impossible. Musk's approach to entrepreneurship is characterized by his willingness to tackle problems others deem insurmountable, whether it's revolutionizing the automotive industry with electric vehicles, making space travel commercially viable, or conceptualizing new forms of transportation such as the Hyperloop. His success can largely be attributed to his ability to envision a future radically different from the present, coupled with the tenacity to bring that vision to life against all odds.

Musk's leadership and business success are also a product of his hands-on approach and attention to detail. He is known for immersing himself in the technical aspects of his companies' projects, often working alongside engineers and designers to solve complex problems. This hands-on involvement not only demonstrates his commitment to his companies' missions but also inspires a culture of hard work and innovation among his employees. Moreover, Musk's ability to think strategically, pivot when necessary, and leverage the synergies between his various ventures has allowed him to build an ecosystem of companies that support and enhance each other's capabilities. Despite facing significant criticism and challenges, including concerns about his management style and the high-pressure environment at some of his companies, Musk's track record of turning groundbreaking ideas into successful businesses continues to solidify his reputation as one of the most influential entrepreneurs of the modern era.

Criticisms of His Leadership

Despite his successes, Musk's leadership style has not been without its detractors. Critics have pointed to several aspects of his management and behavior:

Workplace Culture: Musk's companies, particularly Tesla, have faced criticism over intense work demands placed on employees, leading to concerns about work-life balance and overall employee well-being.

Communication Style: Musk's use of social media and public statements have sometimes led to controversy and legal scrutiny. His tweets have affected stock prices and drawn the attention of regulatory bodies, raising questions about the appropriateness of such communications for a CEO.

Management Decisions: Musk's decision-making and management style have been described as erratic or overly aggressive by some observers. High turnover rates among senior executives in his companies have been attributed to the high-pressure environment and Musk's demanding expectations.

CHAPTER 10: PERSONAL LIFE

Elon Musk's personal life, much like his professional endeavors, is complex and multifaceted, blending private interests, relationships, and family life with his overarching vision for the future. Musk, known for his relentless work ethic and dedication to his companies, also navigates a rich tapestry of personal experiences and interests.

Elon Musk has lived in various places throughout his life, including South Africa, Canada, and the United States. In recent years, Musk has made headlines for his decision to sell most of his real estate holdings as part of a broader vision to simplify his life and focus on his mission to Mars. He has mentioned living in a modest, prefabricated house near SpaceX's facilities in Boca Chica, Texas, reflecting his commitment to his work and the goal of making life multi-planetary.

Relationships and Children

Musk's personal relationships have been as publicized as his business ventures. He has been married and divorced three times, twice to the same woman, English actress Talulah Riley. Musk was also married to Canadian author Justine Wilson, with whom he has five sons: twins Griffin and Xavier, and triplets Damian, Saxon, and Kai. The couple had a first son who tragically died of sudden infant death syndrome (SIDS) at 10 weeks old. Musk has also been in a relationship with Canadian musician Grimes (Claire Boucher), with whom he shares two children, a son named X Æ A-Xii and a daughter named Exa Dark Sideræl Musk. Musk's role as a father is something he occasionally shares glimpses of on social media, portraying moments of family life amidst his bustling schedule.

Hobbies and Interests

Despite his busy professional life, Musk has a variety of interests and hobbies. He is known for his passion for reading, with a particular interest in science fiction and fantasy novels, historical biographies, and books on physics and engineering. These readings have not only provided relaxation but have also inspired some of his business ventures. Musk is also interested in video games, citing them as both a form of entertainment and a window into the potential of technology to create alternate realities.

Musk has expressed interest in art and design, which is reflected in the aesthetics of Tesla's vehicles, SpaceX's spacecraft, and even the unique presentation of Neuralink's product announcements. Additionally, he has a fondness for movies, particularly those in the science fiction genre, which aligns with his futuristic visions.

Given Musk's notorious work schedule, his spare time is limited. However, he has shared that spending time with his children is a priority when he is not working. Musk also occasionally attends high-profile events and engages in social media, where he shares thoughts on a wide range of topics, interacts with fans and critics alike, and provides updates on his companies' projects.

CHAPTER 11: WHAT DOES THE FUTURE HOLD?

Elon Musk's trajectory has always been about challenging the status quo and envisioning a future that many would deem the realm of science fiction. From revolutionizing transportation on Earth and in space to reimagining human interaction with technology, Musk's ambitions are vast. As we look to the future, the plans for his companies promise a continuation of this boundary-pushing journey.

SpaceX and the Dream of Mars

Elon Musk's dream of Mars is not just an ambitious goal for SpaceX but a cornerstone of his vision for the future of humanity. At the core of this vision is the belief that ensuring the survival and flourishing of human civilization necessitates becoming a multi-planetary species. Mars, with its relatively hospitable environment and proximity to Earth, presents the most viable option for establishing a human presence beyond our planet. Musk's plans for Mars colonization are detailed, ambitious, and represent a multi-decade commitment to one of the most complex endeavors humanity may undertake.

SpaceX's strategy for Mars colonization revolves around the development of the Starship spacecraft, which is designed to be fully reusable and capable of carrying large crews and cargo to the Red Planet. The Starship's development is underpinned by SpaceX's innovative approach to rocketry, as demonstrated by the reusability of the Falcon 9 and Falcon Heavy rockets, which significantly reduce the cost of access to space. The Starship takes this a step further, aiming to reduce the cost per ton to Mars to a point where a self-sustaining colony becomes feasible.

The initial missions to Mars are expected to focus on delivering cargo, including the infrastructure necessary for life support, habitats, and fuel production facilities. These missions will lay the groundwork for the first human explorers, who will face the monumental task of establishing a sustainable outpost. Musk has outlined plans for a Mars Base Alpha, a fully functioning settlement on Mars capable of supporting a growing population.

One of the critical components of making life on Mars sustainable is the development of in-situ resource utilization (ISRU) technologies. SpaceX plans to use Mars' natural resources, such as ice and atmospheric carbon dioxide, to produce water, oxygen, and methane fuel. This would enable the refueling of Starships on Mars, making the return journey to Earth feasible and completing the cycle of interplanetary travel.

The timeline for these milestones is aggressive, with Musk suggesting that the first crewed missions to Mars could occur within the next decade. However, the challenges are immense, ranging from the technical hurdles of designing spacecraft and habitats that can support life in the harsh Martian environment, to the physiological and psychological challenges of long-duration space travel and living on another planet.

SpaceX's dream of Mars goes beyond the technical achievement of landing humans on another planet; it embodies a philosophical stance on the future of humanity. Musk envisions a future where humanity's survival is secured through the establishment of a multi-planetary presence, where the human spirit of exploration and curiosity leads us to new frontiers, and where the challenges of living on Mars spur innovations that benefit life on Earth as well.

Tesla's Continued Revolution in Energy and Transport

Tesla's journey under Elon Musk's leadership is not just about producing electric vehicles; it's about sparking a revolution in both energy and transport, fundamentally changing how society powers its mobility and manages its energy needs. Looking towards the future, Tesla aims to continue its expansion and innovation across several fronts, further solidifying its role in the transition to a sustainable energy economy.

The automotive sector will remain a primary focus, with Tesla continually refining its lineup and introducing new models designed to cover more market segments. The potential introduction of a compact EV would mark Tesla's foray into a highly competitive segment, offering a more affordable option and potentially increasing EV adoption globally. Additionally, a high-capacity electric van could cater to the commercial transport sector, emphasizing Tesla's commitment to electrifying all forms of transportation, not just passenger cars. These developments signify Tesla's strategy to make electric vehicles accessible and desirable for every potential car buyer, directly contributing to the reduction of carbon emissions from the transport sector.

Beyond vehicles, Tesla's energy division is poised for significant growth, with the Solar Roof and Powerwall battery storage solutions at its core. The Solar Roof, a product that integrates solar cells directly into roofing tiles, represents a leap towards aesthetically pleasing, efficient solar energy generation for homes. As production scales and installation processes improve, the Solar Roof could become a mainstream option for homeowners seeking to reduce their reliance on traditional energy sources. Meanwhile, the Powerwall and larger-scale Tesla battery products offer the promise of storing renewable energy, ensuring its availability on demand and stabilizing the grid — critical capabilities as the world shifts towards intermittent energy sources like wind and solar.

Tesla's innovations in battery technology and energy storage are also expected to extend beyond residential applications, with implications for utility-scale energy storage and even grid independence. The development of more efficient, cost-effective battery solutions could enable entire communities and cities to operate on renewable energy, reducing the need for fossil fuel-based power generation and enhancing energy security.

Furthermore, Tesla's commitment to sustainability and innovation is also evident in its approach to manufacturing and the supply chain. Musk has hinted at the continuous improvement of manufacturing processes through initiatives like the Gigafactory development, aiming to reduce costs, increase production efficiency, and minimize the environmental impact of battery and vehicle production. These efforts are critical in addressing the growing demand for EVs and energy storage solutions while adhering to Tesla's environmental and sustainability goals.

In the broader scope, Tesla's vision encompasses not only the products it creates but also the influence it exerts on the automotive and energy industries. By proving the viability and profitability of electric vehicles and renewable energy products, Tesla has compelled traditional automakers and energy companies to accelerate their own transitions towards sustainability. This ripple effect, spurred by Tesla's continued innovation and success, contributes to a faster global shift towards cleaner, renewable energy sources.

Neuralink's Quest to Enhance the Human Brain

As Neuralink ventures further into the uncharted territories of neuroscience and technology, its future endeavors promise to fundamentally alter our understanding and interaction with the human brain. Looking ahead, Neuralink aims to pioneer developments that could reshape medicine, enhance human capabilities, and redefine our relationship with artificial intelligence.

In the medical realm, Neuralink's aspirations involve revolutionary treatments for a spectrum of neurological conditions and injuries. The potential to restore lost sensory or motor functions offers a new horizon for individuals affected by spinal cord injuries, Parkinson's disease, epilepsy, and more. Future advancements might allow for the precise modulation of neural circuits, offering targeted therapies for complex conditions like depression or Alzheimer's disease, with minimal side effects compared to current treatments. The ambition extends to creating prosthetics that feel and function like natural limbs, connected and controlled by the brain's neural network.

Beyond therapeutic applications, Neuralink envisions a future where its technology enhances human cognition, memory, and communication. This could manifest in the ability to directly interface with digital devices, offering seamless access to information and new forms of communication that transcend language barriers. Imagine learning a new skill or language instantaneously or sharing thoughts and experiences directly from brain to brain. Such capabilities could revolutionize education, creativity, and how we interact as a society.

Moreover, Neuralink's pursuit of a symbiotic relationship between humans and AI seeks to ensure that humanity can keep pace with rapid advancements in artificial intelligence. This integration could lead to enhanced decision-making processes, by combining human intuition with AI's computational power, potentially unlocking new levels of innovation and problem-solving capabilities.

However, the road ahead for Neuralink is fraught with technical, ethical, and regulatory challenges. Achieving these ambitious goals requires not only groundbreaking scientific discoveries but also navigating the complex landscape of bioethics and public policy. Questions of privacy, autonomy, and the implications of enhanced human capabilities will need to be addressed, ensuring that such advancements benefit society as a whole.

As Neuralink continues to push the boundaries of what is possible, it stands on the cusp of creating a future where the lines between biological and digital intelligence blur. This convergence holds the promise of unlocking untapped human potential, offering profound enhancements to our cognitive and physical capabilities, and possibly even altering the course of human evolution. The future of Neuralink is not merely about technological innovation; it's about reimagining the possibilities of the human condition.

The Boring Company's Impact on Urban Mobility

The future of The Boring Company is poised on the brink of potentially revolutionizing urban and intercity mobility. As it moves from concept to implementation, the company's vision of alleviating congestion through underground tunnel networks could transform the fabric of how we perceive and navigate city landscapes. Looking ahead, The Boring Company aims to not only refine its tunneling technology but also expand its projects to demonstrate the practical applications and benefits of its innovations on a larger scale.

One of the key aspirations for The Boring Company's future is the widespread adoption of its Loop and Hyperloop systems. The Loop system, designed for shorter intra-city commutes, envisions transporting individuals and vehicles at high speeds through tunnels, drastically reducing urban travel times and by-passing surface traffic congestion. As cities continue to grow and traffic becomes increasingly burdensome, the demand for efficient, scalable transportation solutions like the Loop could see a significant rise. The success of pilot projects, such as the Las Vegas Convention Center Loop, serves as a stepping stone towards broader implementation, potentially leading to networks of Loop tunnels beneath major cities around the world.

In parallel, The Boring Company's ambition extends to the development of the Hyperloop — a high-speed transportation system that promises to redefine long-distance travel. With the potential to achieve speeds surpassing those of commercial air travel, the Hyperloop could connect major cities in minutes or hours, fundamentally changing the dynamics of intercity and even international travel. The company's future efforts may focus on advancing the necessary technologies and infrastructure to make the Hyperloop a reality, including addressing the engineering, safety, and regulatory challenges associated with such a ground-breaking transportation system.

Furthermore, The Boring Company's vision for the future includes continuous innovation in tunneling technology. By pioneering faster, more cost-effective methods of tunnel construction, the company seeks to lower the barriers to entry for subterranean transportation projects. These advancements could not only facilitate the expansion of Loop and Hyperloop systems but also inspire new applications for underground infrastructure, from freight transport tunnels to utility corridors, further enhancing urban sustainability and resilience.

However, realizing these ambitious goals will require navigating a complex landscape of technical, regulatory, and societal challenges. The Boring Company will need to demonstrate the safety, efficiency, and environmental benefits of its systems to gain public trust and regulatory approval. Engaging with communities, policymakers, and industry stakeholders will be crucial in aligning the company's innovations with broader transportation and urban planning goals.

The future of The Boring Company holds the promise of a world where traffic congestion is no longer an intractable problem, and where high-speed, efficient travel between and within cities becomes commonplace. By reimagining the possibilities of transportation infrastructure, Elon Musk's venture stands to not only alleviate the stresses of modern urban living but also open up new horizons for human mobility.

A Legacy of Innovation and Challenges

Elon Musk's legacy, as it stands today, is already one of monumental innovation and relentless pursuit of what many considered unattainable. He has fundamentally altered industries, shifted public perspectives on technology and sustainability, and inspired a new generation of entrepreneurs and engineers to dream big. Musk's ventures have redefined the automotive industry with electric vehicles, propelled the commercial space industry into a new era, spearheaded advancements in renewable energy, and are beginning to unravel the complex interface between the human brain and artificial intelligence. His work ethic, vision, and ability to navigate through immense challenges have painted him as a figure whose impact transcends the companies he has built.

Looking forward, if Musk achieves all that he has set out to do, his legacy could stand as a pivotal turning point for humanity. In envisioning a multi-planetary species, Musk is not merely focusing on the survival of humanity but is also instilling a sense of purpose and adventure about our place in the universe. The successful colonization of Mars would represent one of the most significant achievements in human history, echoing the pioneering spirit that has driven humanity's greatest explorations and discoveries.

Within the realm of sustainable energy and transportation, Musk's ambitions could lead to a world where reliance on fossil fuels is a memory, significantly altering the trajectory of environmental degradation. A future where electric vehicles and renewable energy sources are the norm would usher in a new era of clean, efficient energy use, potentially transforming economic, political, and social landscapes worldwide.

Through Neuralink and advancements in brain-machine interfaces, Musk's legacy could also encompass profound shifts in how humans interact with technology, and indeed, what it means to be human. If successful, this technology could revolutionize medicine, enhance human capabilities, and create new modes of communication and interaction, potentially redefining human intellect, creativity, and even consciousness.

Elon Musk's legacy, should he accomplish his wide-ranging goals, could stand as a testament to the power of visionary thinking combined with relentless execution. It would portray a narrative of a man who not only envisioned a future vastly different from the present but also played a pivotal role in its realization. Such a legacy would be characterized by a profound impact on the planet, human society, and our understanding of our place in the cosmos, marking Musk as one of the most influential figures of the 21st century and beyond.

CONCLUSION

In the pages of "Elon Musk: A Biography of an Entrepreneur and Innovator," we have journeyed through the life of one of the most influential and visionary figures of our time. From his early years in South Africa, marked by curiosity and an insatiable appetite for knowledge, to his ascent as a pioneer reshaping industries and challenging our collective imagination, Elon Musk's story is one of relentless pursuit and audacious dreams.

We've explored Musk's initial ventures into the tech world, where companies like Zip2 and X.com laid the groundwork for what would become a monumental career in entrepreneurship. The creation of Tesla Motors and SpaceX — each a testament to Musk's belief in the impossible — highlights not only his role in driving forward electric vehicles and space travel but also his impact on environmental sustainability and humanity's future among the stars.

Through Neuralink, SolarCity, and his innovations in transportation, including the Hyperloop and The Boring Company, Musk has continued to push the boundaries of what technology can achieve. His acquisition of Twitter further underscores his influence on global communication and the digital landscape.

Yet, beyond the entrepreneur and innovator, we've glimpsed the person behind the accomplishments. Musk's philosophy, leadership style, personal life, and the challenges and criticisms he has faced offer a more nuanced understanding of his complex character. His vision for the future, grounded in a blend of optimism and pragmatism, invites us to consider not just the potential of technology, but the responsibility that accompanies its development and use.

As we conclude this biography, it's clear that Elon Musk's journey is far from complete. The final chapter — "What Does the Future Hold?" — reminds us that Musk's ambitions stretch into the decades to come, with goals that could further revolutionize our world. His legacy, already substantial, is poised to grow as he continues to pursue projects that could redefine human existence.

"Elon Musk: A Biography of an Entrepreneur and Innovator" has endeavored to capture the essence of a man driven by the desire to solve humanity's most pressing problems through innovation and ingenuity. In doing so, it invites readers to reflect on the power of vision, the importance of perseverance, and the potential within each of us to effect meaningful change. Elon Musk's story is not just an account of personal and professional triumphs; it is a call to action for future generations to dream big, challenge the status quo, and venture boldly into the unknown.